# CRAZY HAS A NAME

## Breaking the Stigma Placed on Mental Disorders

by

**SHELIA R. HOLLAWAY**

Paperback ISBN: 978-1-963250-35-0

Hardcover ISBN: 979-8-218278-48-9

Print Illusion by Anthony Walls

This book is dedicated

To those mothers who have lost a child forever. To those mothers who have spent countless nights wondering where their child might be. To those mothers who have repeatedly cried out for help only to have another door closed. And to the parent who did not get to hear the "WHY."

You are not alone.

LaMar

You left your mother with an unimaginable task. You said, "I'm giving you my journaling; maybe you could find a use for them. And never forget that I love you and will be with you always. You were the best mother; never forget that."

Son, your words of comfort gave me the strength to complete such a task.

Rest in peace, my love.

# MENTAL HEALTH *Champion*

Thank you so much for being a Mental Health Champion! Your support serves as an inspiration for everyone who has been impacted by mental health. You truly are a beacon of hope.

## PLATINUM LEVEL

**PASTOR FRED** HARRIS

**LADY SHERRY M.** DONAHUE BROWN, M.ED

**DR. DOLORES** KING-JACKSON
**MR. HUGH** JACKSON

**RAYMOND** R SHIRLEE

**PAUL & PATRICIA** RHODES

**JOHN** HOLLAWAY

**RENEE** WARD

**SONJI** PATMON

*Symphony Auto Spa*
**BRANDON** POINTER

**THE MAJOR FUNERAL HOME**

**KASANDRA** PHILLIPS

**NETRA & TY** FITZGERALD

**ASHLEY GREEN**-FAGAN

**BRIDGET** CHATMAN

**KATHY** JONES

**KIM** JERNIGAN

**TOMMIE & VERNON M.** CONWAY JR.

**RON & LISA** WILLIAMS

**DR. KIMBERLY** UDELL, DO

KING'S COFFEE
**MAJOR (RET.) ERIC K.** KING, US ARMY

**EDWARD** JONES

**FIELDING & BEATRICE** WILSON

## GOLD LEVEL

**LEONARD & PAULA** HALL

## SILVER LEVEL

**LASHONDA** HOLMES **CARY & CHRISTI** SHADY **CARMEN & JACQUES** DILONGA **LASHUNDA** HATTER

# ACKNOWLEDGMENTS

First, I give honor to my Lord and Savior, Jesus Christ.

In you, I found Courage.

---

So many people love me, and I am so grateful. I want to express my gratitude to all of you. To the best family, you guys are always present. I love you.

To my spiritual leaders, Pastor and Sister Dwight Mckissic Sr, Pastor Fred Harris, and Mother Harris. Thank you for always supporting me.

To Glorian Ford, Kasandra Phillips, and Anshera James. Thank you for always answering my phone calls, editing my words, and never saying “No.” I appreciate you.

To Anthony Walls, when I was searching for an artist to get my vision for the Crazy Has A Name book cover, you nailed it. Thank you.

To the late Donna Freeman, Carutha Braden, Breulah Hollaway, and my mom, Essie Tappin. Thank you for your wisdom, sacrifices, work ethic, and unconditional love. I will forever carry you in my heart.

Finally, to the remarkable men who carry LaMar's memories in their hearts. Herman Davis Jr., Charles Hollaway Sr. and Jr., and my son, Herman Davis III (Trey). Thank you for constantly checking on me.

# FOREWORD

As a therapist, I have spent my days, months, and years listening to stories. They are in constant transition, making an impact, leaving scars, detouring dreams, and altering generations. All of them have had a significant influence on me. This story is no different.

In my 30-year career, I have had the honor of helping people, giving hope, and, at times, walking through difficult seasons. In this journey, I have come to realize that the human experience is unique. As we are all walking next to each other in this life, I've realized that although we have common experiences, we reference different stories. We make decisions out of lived experiences and essential relationships. We communicate, connect, and cohabitate in places that may seem in unity but often are vastly different.

Mental Health is a certain science, at times with an uncertain display. Our bodies and words often mimic what is accepted and acknowledged as normal.

However, neurologically, emotionally, and psychologically, some are imprisoned by its tormenting thoughts. Individuals who endure are often seen as having behavioral abnormalities and are ignored or pushed to the corners of society. Unseen and unheard. The complexity of care and the taboo of the label of mental illness have unfortunately placed many in the unrelenting cycle of enduring its effects and medicating them. This contributes to substance abuse, homelessness, self-harm and suicide.

This raw account of a mother's love for her son is a gift. Shelia passionately tells her story while detailing her journey of crushing grief and liberating love. Her strength and courage is inspiring and hopeful. She willingly allows us into intimate places so we can see and experience the misery of losing a child and the exuberance of letting him go.

I can recommend this resource because Shelia has done the work of reaching deep inside and telling the painful story of love and liberation. She allows us to sit in a front-row seat to consume the writings of her son in his own words while noting their impact and torturous effects. This kind of courage and open access is what we need in order to begin an honest conversation in the care of those living with mental illness and the anguish of those who love them.

Shundria Riddick M.A., LPC

# Table of Contents

# CHAPTER 1

## Letter To Mom

# BREAKING

## THE STIGMA

## Myth #1

*Mental illnesses aren't real or legitamite.*

79% agree that mental health disorders are real **conditions.** Only 45-51% of people in developed countries believe that mental illness is similar to physical illness. But these diseases are as real as any other health **problem.** They can result from genetics, abnormal brain chemistry, substance abuse, or in response to trauma or abuse.

“ ”

www.etactics.com

Burned into my memory, leaving its footprints to dance across my mind. It was so busy that day in the salon. The phone just continued to ring, and I finally answered it. Hello, I remember saying hello and hearing the voice of the police officer speaking, but I could not quite understand, or maybe I did not process what was being said. It was on my cell phone roughly around 7:30 P.M., and I had been working all day preparing for my vacation. We were headed to Belize; we were so excited to go. I remember the sound of silent chaos chattering in my right ear, and my entire left side went numb. What did you say? Will you please repeat that? Are you calling the right number? Who are you looking for? I remember hearing the enormously sounding thud of my racing heart as the pressure behind my eyes became increasingly present.

A cold stillness crept across my face, and a feeling of anxiety moved in as I heard the voice ask if LaMar Davis was my son but did not answer. Perhaps, I thought if I stayed quiet, the inevitable truth would refrain from entering the atmosphere. After three attempts to get me to admit that I was indeed LaMar's mom, something in his tone sent chills down my spine. I was frozen, frozen in time. I could not breathe. Sometimes, I can still feel that same chill. It appears it lurks and waits for its opportunity to be acknowledged through my grief, who invites it in.

The officer proceeded to utter from his mouth, "I'm sorry, but your son committed suicide." Suddenly, time stood still, and everything was now moving in slow motion. My words were dragging, but my mind was racing, and I could not catch up. I asked him why he did that. How do you know that? Where is he? Who was there with him? I think I went deaf for a moment and could not hear anything he was saying to me. I was inundated with disbelief; this could not be true. The only sound I could hear was like an explosion; it was an involuntary screeching, growling scream released from my soul, and it pierced my heart. What is this? How can this be happening? He continued to talk, telling me that my son, my sweet baby, was lying in the morgue. LaMar had his picture ID and an envelope with the writing "To my mother, please call her" in his pocket, and that is when I knew this was not a dream.

I dropped the phone and raised my head, and the once vibrant, lively room was now filled with the lifeless bodies of my clients. I did not know what to do; I was paralyzed. I asked my assistant to call my co-worker to ask if she could come and finish my clients, but she was unavailable. I had no choice but to pull myself together. I managed to walk over to my station. I could not see my baby, and my job was to finish styling my client's hair. The room was so quiet; it was as if even the air had vanished, and it wasn't easy to breathe. I remember thinking, what do I do? Who should I be calling? I have got to finish my client's hair.

*Holding back tears, I managed to call my big sister. Not thinking where she might be or what she might be doing, she began to scream and cry out loud."*

Holding back tears, I managed to call my big sister. Not thinking where she might be or what she might be doing, she began to scream and cry out loud. I remember thinking, "Oh my, what did I just do?" I immediately began to console her, then asked her to tell our mother in person and get here as fast as possible.

Just as I finished the last client, my husband and other son were arriving to take me home. I do not quite remember the ride. I was lost as to why my baby did this to himself, to me, and to us. I thought he was in a good place in his life. We had completed a six-month rehabilitation program, and he was back at the University; it was his junior year. I just talked to him the day before; he was scheduled to house- sit while his dad and I were on vacation. Nothing in his voice or conversation led me to believe he was hurting inside and certainly not about to harm himself.

I called the police department. I desperately needed closure as to why my son killed himself. I had to hear him tell me in his own words. I was transferred to the homicide division, and I was told they could not release his belongings because the case was still open, but they would make a copy of the letter for me. I hurried to the station. When I arrived, I was told to have a seat and that someone would be right with me. It seemed like a lifetime; thirty minutes had passed, and still, no one had come to greet me. Finally, a young detective stood before me and introduced himself; he took a breath and sat beside me. I started to cry. What a compassionate, empathetic man he was. He shared with me that he understood where I was and how I was feeling because his brother committed suicide the year before. He went on to say that his mother sat in the same position as I was last year due to his brother's battle with mental illness. For him to release the letter to me, I had to promise to wait until I got home to read it, I promised. This was no coincidence; my wait was long, but the timing was perfect to have the right detective come to comfort me.

This had to be the longest drive home. As I kept glancing at the unopened envelope, my imagination was dominating my mind, and I could not control my urge to open it. Finally, I made it home. I opened the door to my home, and eerie, still quietness was in the air. My husband had not made it home from work yet, and a small voice inside told me to wait, yet a mother's love told me to read my baby's letter.

I held the envelope in my hands, and I slowly opened it, and my fingertips were touching the last words written by my son. I unfolded the trifold, and my eyes started to tear up. I had the most devastating yet beautiful opportunity to hear from the heart of my beloved baby.

The letter read...

Mom,

I love you so much, and I am so sorry for what I've put you through. You were such a wonderful mother. This is a personal choice that I have made for myself. This has nothing to do with you or a girl or drugs or whatever crazy stupid thing you and everyone else has already assumed. I did this for me. Most people live there lives being as close to happy as they can and experience pockets of time when they feel at their utmost, extreme worst. But my whole life I experienced pockets of happiness while living the vast majority of my life feeling terrible inside. It doesn't make sense, there's no reason for it, I've lived a good life, never wanted for anything really. I'm just tired of fighting so hard to feel what everybody feels normally. I'm sorry, but it's time that I stop riding the fence on this issue. I know you are a strong person, you'll survive this. Give my love and farewells to the family. Tell Trey I said that I'll be watchin and I can't wait till the day comes and becomes the man he is meant to be, make him promise to do that for me.

I love you mother. your son
— Lamon Dennard Davis

How do we accomplish peace in such a tumultuous state of being? When my heart is overwhelmed, when do I find rest? I have never blamed you for who you are, but I have blamed myself for not seeing your pain. What could I have done to process the idea of losing myself? My blood flowing through your veins has abruptly stopped its course, and your soul has been freed. Why do I feel imprisoned by this grief when you have liberated yourself from the bondage you were held captive to? My love, my heart, my peace, my strength, my hope, my admiration, my everything. Am I being selfish? I do not know the order of my thoughts, and my steps have slowed to a crawl. Why didn't I wait to read this letter? Would I have fewer questions if your dad was here? I am alone, I am alone. This black hole of uncertainty has consumed all my consciousness, and I cannot feel the bottom of my feet as I paced across the floor. Wavering back and forth, tears and laughter, a confused mentality is now my reality. My sweet boy has transitioned into his peace, and I cannot stand this pain.

# CHAPTER 2

# They Call It Crazy

# BREAKING

## THE STIGMA

## *Myth #2*

*I don't know anyone with a mental health condition.*

In the US, one in five adults and 13-20% of children will experience a diagnosable mental health disorder in any given year. One in four college students has a diagnosable condition. Since these are such common conditions, you most likely know someone experiencing a disorder. Or, you may experience one someday.

" "

www.etactics.com

What is crazy? This word has become a stigma on people from all walks of life. It is non- gender specific, not limited to ethnic backgrounds, and has no age requirement. The word crazy is defined as mentally deranged. "Stella went crazy and assaulted a visitor," extremely enthusiastic, "I'm crazy about Cindy." (Google) Merriam-Webster states: Full of cracks or flaws, not mentally sound, marked by thought or action that lacks reason, "yelling like a crazy man," impractical, erratic, unusual, absurdly fond, obsessed, and the list goes on.

> *"Society is misguided and under-informed, and our lack of know-ledge has limited our capacity to understand the difference bet-ween intolerable behavior and mental disorders"*

Society is misguided and underinformed, and our lack of knowledge has limited our capacity to understand the difference between intolerable behavior and mental disorders. Often, those affected by mental illness (a chemical imbalance in the brain) are oblivious to their complete thought process and are ill-equipped to weigh the potential impact and/or consequences of their behavior. Moreover, the persistent need for a sense of normalcy is increasingly present.

Looking back, I remember my son saying, "Mom, I don't know why sometimes I feel happy, then I feel sad," total opposite. I did not know how to respond as I had no prior exposure to mental illness or chemical discrepancies. There was no proper introduction to these uncommon names: Bipolar, Manic Depression, or Schizophrenia.

Prayer. I placed prayer oil on my son's head and prayed for him as he slept. Something was occurring that was much larger than me, and I knew I had to place this in capable hands. I gave it to the hand of God. I asked God to afford him peace, understanding, hope, and joy and to reassure him that he was loved. I longed for LaMar to be who he was created to be.

A stranger crept into an unrecognizable being and consumed LaMar. One morning, he came home from class reeking of alcohol—musky, pungent, and overbearing, I was surprised to see him in the morning and smelling of alcohol at that time of day. He had been so overwhelmed in trying to locate an elusive, entangled thought of being routine that he habituated to self-medicate.

I reacted in a very stern, black mama way. "Boy sit your butt down and tell me what's going on with you," I said. He responded, "Mom, the voices are getting louder in my head." I immediately got up and called the doctor, and she responded by telling me to get him in right away. It was not until the following day, when we saw our family physician, we both began to understand what was happening inside my son's head.

This was one of the most challenging encounters I have ever had to work through as a mother. Our doctor asked a series of uncomfortable questions like: Have you ever tried to hurt yourself? How often do you hear the voices, and how many are there? Can you imagine what it felt like to hear my son mumble the answers? Tears poured down my face as he told her an instance of the voices instructing him to go to the freeway bridge and jump. He said the only reason he did not jump was that he knew his mother loved him. LaMar was diagnosed with Major Depressive Disorder, Anxiety, Dysthymia, ETOH Abuse Disorder, and Multi Somatoform Disorder.

The chemical imbalance in his brain was desperately trying to find its balance, and this was one of the reasons he turned to drugs and alcohol. LaMar was prescribed trial doses of Lexapro and Klonopin. At this moment, it became more evident why he became addicted to this undeniable lifestyle. We were urged to be cautious of combining the medication with alcohol as it will intensify its effect and can become dangerous. She further explained drinking alcohol acted much like the medication, except it is short-acting while the medication serves and treats for a longer duration.

Pause, just for a moment. Process this newness and what it means. Hold your demeanor and be steadfast in this hour. Keep the faith and trust in God. My mind was reminding my body to breathe as I fought to keep my composure in front of LaMar. I had to be his rock, his foundation of truth, as he has now allowed himself to be vulnerable enough to share his. I was so proud of him for affording us the opportunity to become more aware. It must have been a steep hill to climb, an unadulterated feat.

Once we got home, LaMar rushed to do some research on the computer. What an incredible mind my son had, an exuberant, intelligent man. He hurried over to me with photos in tow, normal brain tissue and chemically imbalanced. He boldly and assuredly explained, "Mom, this is why I will never be normal," the picture showed waves of consistent highs and lows, representing his emotions.

The chemicals responsible for controlling the brain's functions are called neurotransmitters and include noradrenaline, serotonin, and dopamine—big words for the emotion of happy or sad. I was in awe of how this could happen to such an intelligent child. Every waking moment, my baby experiences pockets of sadness, then happiness, sadness, then happiness, a repeat cycle. A sense of helplessness invaded my being as I could not do anything but allow this process to happen. I needed my mother, she needed to know what was happening with LaMar.

I dialed my mother's number, and with each tone, I felt like I was falling into a sea of uncertainty, and it was becoming harder and harder to stay afloat. She picked up the phone, and I shared the sad news. To my surprise, it did not surprise her. She said, "Girl, that's what Mama had before she died." I could not believe what I heard, and I was numb and mad. This did not make sense; why wouldn't this have been important enough to share with me and my siblings? Back then, there were no medical terms used, only the word **crazy,** so how could she share something she could not explain?

We later learned this was believed to be hereditary, a genetic predisposition. This illness skipped my generation and adhered to my son. A blessing in disguise? I was tasked with helping my son, and I was determined to provide all the support I could to ensure him a well-lived life.

The dear doctor stated to my son and me that, at this time, no one drug could be prescribed to LaMar that would cure him. All our doctor could do was start him on one medication and monitor him for six months to see if it was therapeutic. The plan was to utilize the approach of trial and error. Once again, I was heartbroken, knowing my son was suffering inside, only to be told he would be experimented on like a guinea pig.

Guide me, oh Lord, wrap your arms around us and carry us through this storm. Please help us to maintain our peace as you provide provision for our seemingly destitute path. We are seeking your wisdom and leaning on your word. God, heal this pain, free him from his solemnly agonizing sadness, and renew his mind. Transform this illness into freedom unseen. Allow him the strength to fight this and to conclude with a victory. Throughout our dismay and subdued witness, let us become more aware of your presence and be filled with your peace as it surpasses all understanding. Continue to be our everything and increase in us while removing fear. Remind us that we are servants only to you and not to our circumstances. Nothing happens by chance, as you are the author and finisher of creation and all it has to say. We shall not perish by the wayside as you are the way, the truth, and the life! We give you honor in this time of need and praise you unconditionally. Amen

This was my prayer as I tangled my tattered hope with a strand of promise, and I sprinkled it with just a little more faith to press forward. There was no room for fear, no time to tarry. We were on a mission for total healing. We had to become everything to defeat this giant or at least understand it.

I had to recondition my habit of understanding that my son was not crazy. He had a chemical imbalance in his brain, in which he had no control, nor did he ask for it.

# CHAPTER 3

# LaMar

# BREAKING

## THE STIGMA

## *Myth #3*

***Children don't have mental health disorders.***

As of 2015, over 17 million children in the US had a psychiatric disorder. In any given year, one-fifth of American children receive a mental health diagnosis. But they can be difficult to identify in children since they often have different symptoms than adults. Age can make it complicated for them to explain why they're acting a certain way.

"I am prepared to die at any time. That statement should not be misconstrued, I don't want to die, at least not right now, or even soon, for that matter. But I do not fear death. It is a considerable outcome in all that I do, but dying to me would be one amazing adventure that I would be happy to embark on at any moment. I just can't shake the feeling that something is not right in this world. I look around as if through my eyes I have seen it all before. As if through my eyes that I have been exposed to this world of lies, deceit, greed, hate, and jealousy. Although I may or may not have been exposed to those things and then some, I feel as if none of that is new; in fact, that's why I hate the news the most, it reports on the same thing day in and day out.

Violence, poverty, death, and destruction. I've seen it, but I haven't seen it. I know it, but I don't know it. It is as though I have been here before, I'm sick of it. It's either that or there is a piece of my soul that remembers being in a place where all was right in the world. Perhaps all the disdain and disgust that I harbor toward this world is a result of a part of me that cannot let go of a better life than I once knew.Or perhaps, a connection that I have with the spiritual world allows me to know what bliss feels like, and my physical self responds with a negative feeling toward everything here in this imperfect world."

It's a gift, a wonderful place to be in—the mind of my child whom I have loved so dearly from the moment of conception. I have longed for a moment to remember and think of love again. I hope that you, and I, will learn, grow, try, fail, learn, and live. I cannot begin to tell you the thought process that has entered my mind from rereading a piece of the Journal of my son's mind. Is it something that is welcomed, or is this something that I should set aside? I have long hoped for an opportunity to relive a moment with my dearly departed LaMar. In his Journal, he has gifted us with the tools and the knowledge base to identify and treat mental illness. The highs, the lows, and the in-betweens. He has given us the most unique, phenomenal piece of work, pure genius.

> *I remember teaching my children to Journal at a young age, I never would have imagined they would have continued this throughout their higher education and even into their personal lives outside of school."*

I remember teaching my children to Journal at a young age, I never would have imagined they would have continued this practice throughout their higher education and even into their personal lives outside of school. I am honored to know that my children took heed to the fantastic world of literature. Being able to leave their mark on this world and understand its impact. I didn't think that this year, 2020, I would be rereading the writings of such an amazing person I have engraved in my heart for eternity. My precious son has allowed us a peek into his mind. Not everything was terrible, not everything was solemn, there were good times, there were joyous occasions, but he was stricken and with these pockets of happiness. Only in a time did he see and feel what we take for granted. A thought process that limited his ability to feel what is thought to be expected. As you read in the above Journal, he was prepared to die anytime. Now, we can take that in a variety of ways. My perception of that statement is he was prepared. He had a realization that allowed him the knowledge and acceptance of his reality.

A beautiful, somber, heartfelt painting. These writings have become one of the world's most prolific and wonderfully orchestrated bodies of work. I like to think of these journals as organ donation. My son gave us something that is not easily obtained. We have been allowed to hear from the mouth of someone who has been silenced by an illness that is not widely accepted or understood. It is the goal of this gift to provide those who have become entirely speechless with a voice. If I needed a kidney transplant, I would be placed on a donor list. My son donated to this community, a glimpse into the thought process of someone suffering from what cannot be seen. It isn't easily diagnosed; it isn't quickly treated. There are so many trials and errors and guessing and treatment options. This is the most insightful, omnibus, education-filled piece of literature I have ever seen.

"I wonder what it is exactly that I am meant to do? Perhaps nothing. The question is not one of choice. If there is a task for this life of mine, I wholeheartedly accept it, which is probably why I'm here in the 1st place. A part of me that existed before birth agreed to be born in order to do something here on earth. The problem is, that my biological mechanism lacks the details of said mission. Somewhere between death and life, I have forgotten what I'm supposed to do. My duty now is to merge the body with the mind with the soul, which most likely still retains that knowledge. That fact was also most likely explained to me before arriving. What sort of thing is so important that I would agree to it, yet knowingly step into this jungle that we call life or being alive as a man? There are tools here, skills that are learned, and even instincts coded into the DNA. Yet the thing to do with them escapes me. Or perhaps I'm insane, and everything I just said is entirely fictional! Time will tell. Tick tock."

How do we measure time? When do we know it's time to do anything? Are we under the same restraints as a 12-hour Clock or a 24-hour Clock? Who decides what time means and where it's supposed to lead us? If, by time, we can configure ourselves to the thought process of someone else's idea of it, will we ever arrive? Some of us have deep-rooted thoughts, others are more superficial. When do we become the metronome? Keeping the rhythm steady? How do we decide what our purpose is? I've often wondered what my world would be like with just one more moment in time. Of course, I'd have to make sure that my timing was in alignment with his so that we could spend our last few seconds together. Was this something that was profoundly executed? Just the fluidity of the strokes of the pen has me in awe of him. He was on to something.

Did you know that creative people are commonly among the most clinically diagnosed as depressed? Were you aware that geniuses were considered schizophrenic? All these creative facets in life have brought us to this point, and now we have a fantastic mind to study. Just from the penmanship and punctuation of these journals written by my son, we have opened a new book, sharing the life of a misplaced soul. He mentions that he was unaware or somehow forgot what he was sent here to do. His purpose is becoming more and more apparent as we continue to dive into some of these works. I refer to them as works because they are truly profound. I am honored to have been left with these insatiable, tantalizing, unwavering truths. These are tools, every word written by someone who knew that he was meant to do and to be something. He mentioned his biological mechanism, lacking the details of his mission. He knew that somewhere between life and death, something was misplaced; we found it.

"If you have a good idea, a beneficial idea, a useful idea, but never share it, express it, or remember it for that matter, is it still a good idea? Was that idea, realization, or revelation even worth the time it took to manifest? "

Do you see how his mind was always fresh? Never a dull moment. There was never a time when he didn't have something to say. Whether it be verbal, something that he had written in his Journal, or something that he had spoken in his mind, he always put forth helpful information. Not all his thoughts were in word formation; sometimes, they were illustrations, actions, and behaviors. He always had something to say. Communication is impeccable. Some of us use sign language, read lips, and read Braille, while others choose to write. I find it easier to communicate after I have written it down. It isn't always easy to verbalize how you might feel and expose yourself audibly. Just like there are many ways to learn something new, there are a plethora of ways to communicate.

> *Hearing is only half the battle in effective communication, we must also learn to listen. Listening does not just come from the ears; it is with every part of your being."*

Hearing is only half the battle in effective communication, we must also learn to listen. Listening does not just come from the ears; it is with every part of your being. When a newborn has soiled its diaper and cannot speak, we utilize our other senses to seek out the problem. We can smell it. It's the same with any other form of practical and active listening. Being engaged with whom you are communicating with is crucial, and tapping into your Critical Thinking Skills is a requirement to obtain an optimal level of communication.

Learning to recognize and ask the right questions is one of the critical components of gainful knowledge. Looking into the mind of someone who may not understand its brain wave pattern is a little more trying and can become exhausting if it is not nurtured and cultivated. Self-care is vital to overcoming any obstacle, especially one that cannot be controlled easily. Remind ourselves that if we do not have the correct approach, our delivery may be distorted, and we can lose focus on our goal.

Be careful not to take offense to reactionary processes as they may not be warranted but could be a coping mechanism for the other party. For every action, there is a reaction. I have learned to COPE: Care, Observe, Prepare, Execute.

**C: Care**

Always show genuine concern and care for the person or situation.

**O: Observe**

Be available, observe body language and any signs of discomfort

**P: Prepare**

Pause and prepare your questions and or responses silently before speaking prematurely

**E: Execute**

Follow through with your completed thought and execute your delivery of information.

# CHAPTER 4

# The Journey

# BREAKING
## THE STIGMA

## *Myth #4*

*People cannot overcome mental illness.*

Only 7% of people in developed countries believed that someone could overcome mental illness. However, most people who experience a mental health problem do recover or can live with and manage their condition. This is especially true for those who get help early. Most people can experience relief with a treatment plan.

" "

www.etactics.com

It felt like I plunged into a darkness with no hope for light. My stomach was full of knots and a quickening of butterflies. Are my feet moving? Am I standing still? I feel stuck, rooted where I had not been planted. I was suddenly cold; I was shivering, and my teeth were chattering. I clenched my jaw and tried to slow the movement in my body. My legs were heavy, weighted down with grief. I had to muster up the strength to take the first step to allow this inevitable journey to begin.

I can remember opening the door and feeling like an intense burst of air almost knocked me over, as if I were in a movie, and I had the lead role. There was no script for what I would endure, and I did not know how to prepare for what was to come. All I could do was allow this natural yet premature course of events to happen. I had no control.

This had to be the longest night of my life. My mind was racing with thoughts of the police officer saying, "You can't see your son until a funeral home picks him up." What funeral home do I call? I've never had to pick a funeral home; this had never happened to me before. I began to ask around, and two funeral home names kept coming up. One was African-American, and the other was white-owned; of course, I gravitated to the African-American-owned establishment. I called and told them my son died, and he was in the morgue waiting to be picked up. I went on to explain I wanted to see him before they touched him, and I didn't care what his appearance looked like. Most of the day went by, and still no response, I was freaking out. I needed to see my baby. I needed to make sure that this was indeed my son.

Finally, I got a call from the funeral home. When can I see my son? Would it be right away? I wanted to see my sweet boy, my baby, right away. By this time, my family had made it to Texas from Arkansas. So, we all jumped in our cars and headed to the funeral home.

Freshly cleaned, the staff draped white sheets around his head and body. As I drew closer to my son's lifeless body, I could feel my legs buckling underneath me. With my husband and surviving son close to my side, I had no idea what we would see. I didn't care. All I wanted was to see and feel my child.

LaMar was lying still, his eyes gently closed as if he were sleeping. To my surprise, I saw peace, peace all over my son's narrow face. No swelling, no apparent wounds or dismemberment, no discoloration, just peace. I began to search for a reason, looking all around under the sheets, overwhelmed with disbelief that my baby boy was dead, dead, never to move again. He had shot himself right above the left temple. The bullet went straight through his brain, exiting out, leaving a small hole on the right side of his head. I draped myself across his body and wept. I hadn't seen him look so at peace in a long time. It warmed my heart so much that I didn't want the funeral home to embalm him. Just let him stay as beautiful as he is right now.

The funeral home staff informed us that embalming was not required by law, but if we wanted the public to view LaMar, I had to allow them to embalm him. I struggled with the decision to embalm because he was perfect, just as he was at that moment. With the influence of family and friends, I wanted to give them an opportunity to see him for the closure they needed. But, as far as I was concerned, everyone who needed to see him was already in that room. After some time, I finally agreed to embalming because I didn't want to seem or be selfish.

The next day was a nightmare! LaMar's father had not made it to town until the following day, so my girlfriend and I accompanied him to the funeral home to see our son. As if this wasn't difficult enough, the person who embalmed my son had him looking like something out of a horror movie. I was speechless for half a second, dumbfounded even. I was in disbelief this wasn't my child. Who is this? This couldn't be my LaMar, his face was all swollen with pockets of fluid all over his face. I went off! One would say I laid my religion down that day. My son was perfect yesterday; what happened? The response one of the staff members said blew me away, "Well, you know he did shoot himself in his head." Yes, I know, and he was shot in the head yesterday, and he didn't look like that!

Words cannot express how angry I was at myself because I knew in my heart that the peace LaMar had on his face was not to be disturbed, yet I gave permission to embalm. I was angry because they took away his peace. I was angry because his father never got a chance to see the peace I saw. I was angry because there was no empathy shown by the very people, I had paid in full the day before to take care of my child. The following day, I called my funeral director to ask if they could fix LaMar. She asked what was wrong with him. All I had gone through the previous day; she knew nothing about it. Oblivious. I was infuriated that my funeral director didn't know my son's peace was taken away. I remember saying, "If you don't fix him, I will not show him, I will not pay you, and I will take it further."

What I know for sure is if you take a picture of a haircut to a stylist and ask for that cut, and they agree to cut that style then turn around and give you a different cut, there is no way for you to achieve that original style, but someone else can make it look presentable. And that's what I got for my LaMar.

> *Another embalmer came in and made him look presentable. I could not mourn the death of my son for making sure the funeral home staff did their job."*

Another embalmer came in and made him look presentable. I could not mourn the death of my son for making sure the funeral home staff did their job. I can never get that moment back, it was lost in time, virtually stolen.

On the day of the viewing, there were wall-to-wall people there. I was amazed to see so many people who loved my son, not only his peers but their parents as well. Amid the storytelling, from so many who stood and spoke their fun memories, the Holy Spirit spoke to me and said get up and talk about Bipolar Disease. At first, I paid no attention, again, louder this time, "GET UP AND TALK ABOUT BIPOLAR DISEASE." I looked around, and I saw all those who loved LaMar. I was uncomfortable with public speaking, so I decided no, I was not doing it. For the third time, even more present, "GET UP AND TALK ABOUT BIPOLAR DISEASE."

I called my beloved friend over, who was directing the order of the service, and whispered, "I'm going to have the last words." Her response was, "Are you sure?". I wanted to scream, "No! My son is lying alone, lifeless in a casket", but I trusted the voice inside. I walked up to the podium with my son and husband on each side. As I began by saying, my son suffered from Bipolar Depression; the more I talked, the less I could hear myself. To this day, I cannot tell you what I shared with all those people. Once the viewing was over, people came around to give their condolences, and everyone was either thanking me for talking about Bipolar or sharing their stories with me. I looked around for my family, but I saw no one, only people lined up all the way out the door, waiting to thank me for talking about Bipolar. At that moment, I looked up and said, "Lord, this isn't about me or LaMar."

The next day at the memorial, people still approached me, sharing their personal stories. What I knew for sure was I didn't volunteer to be in this space. I wanted my son alive and free from the disease that haunted him and caused him to kill himself. But, in reality, I knew I must continue to help as many parents, especially moms with young sons, recognize and understand the signs of Manic Depression. When discussing LaMar's journey, I always start with the sentence, "My son committed suicide," which opens the door to talk about bipolar disorder freely.

I had previously told the funeral home I wanted to witness my son's cremation. They were surprised because no one had ever asked to see their loved one get cremated. I wanted to make sure that my baby was indeed the person being cremated, and I wanted to be with him until the very end. After what I went through earlier, I also didn't trust that I would get my LaMar. I chose cremation because, for so long, my child lived in darkness, and I couldn't bear the thought of putting him in the cold, dark ground and covering him with piles of dirt. Yet, watching him go in that furnace broke me way down. I couldn't show it on the outside; loved ones were present who were having a tough time, and someone had to be strong; in my spirit, I knew it had to be me.

When weakness overwhelms your strength, where do you find power? How can I carry this load on my shoulders when the weight of the world has caused me to succumb? My somber seclusion has enveloped my will. How do I break free from this bondage of responsibility to be the anchor, the pillar of hope and strength? An opportunity to purge is not present, it's all bottled inside. I've held the eruption of emotions for the sake of those more susceptible to the cross I bear. Why has this become my burden? Maybe this is my gift. Why have I been entrusted with such an excellent task? My greatest fear has become my new reality. From beauty to ashes, my son's soul is at rest.

# CHAPTER 5

## Back To The Beginning

# BREAKING

## THE STIGMA

## *Myth #5*

### *I can't help someone who struggles with mental health.*

Showing support is actually key for someone who is struggling. Stigma is such a common reason why people don't receive care. But showing that you care can help reduce this stigma so they're more inclined to get help. Referring them to helpful resources or professional help can also benefit them if they don't know where to seek help.

“ ”

www.etactics.com

"I'm giving you my journaling; maybe you could find a use for them." A quote from LaMar's second letter addressed "Mom." Alone with instructions on how to handle his last affairs. This act of kindness did not surprise me. This was an example of my son's heart—making his bed, cleaning his apartment, leaving money to pay his outstanding debts, and taking his life in the parking lot. LaMar knew that if anyone he loved discovered his remains, they would have to endure the lifelong pain after seeing his lifeless body still in a pool of blood. To the very end, my son cared about everyone else.

On March 9, 1984, I was lying on a surgical table waiting for a cesarean section. An operation by which a fetus is taken from the uterus by cutting through the walls of the abdomen and uterus. A brave, yet scared, twenty-one-year-old mother of one beautiful baby boy was anxiously awaiting the arrival of her second son. Tick-tock. Finally, at 7:40 A.M., a beautiful, chocolate, seven-pound, ten- ounce baby genius entered the world.

I knew, at first sight, LaMar was unique. He had a lighter shade of brown straight down the center of his face. An exuberance of light shined from the inside out. He was an easy baby and hardly ever cried. As a toddler, he didn't have to be entertained, he amused himself. Always taking things apart and putting them back together.

Growing up, school lessons came super easy for LaMar, always looking to be challenged on something new. English and grammar were his things, and he got a kick out of correcting you if you used bad English. He'd probably correct me right now. Quite often, this infuriated most adults because they didn't like being shown up by a child. I remember sitting LaMar down and explaining why the adults reacted negatively when he was trying to be helpful.

One Mother's Day, LaMar asked his dad to take him to Radio Shack to buy me a gift. He found a small audio picture frame, put his picture in it, and recorded his voice, saying, "Happy Mother's Day mom, I love you, and I appreciate all you have done for me over the years." This made me smile the most, mainly because he was only six years old. I wonder sometimes if, in the back of his mind, he knew many years later, that gift would remain the most precious tangible possession I own. Throughout his years, his heart never wavered; he loved giving self-made gifts, helping others, and showing kindness, respect, and love, especially to the girls. LaMar was witty, charming, and extremely intelligent.

In high school, I wanted LaMar to play in the band. His grandfather was a trumpet player, and I felt he, too, had that talent. He often reminded me the band was too slow, not challenging enough, and most of the pretty girls were watching and cheering the sports teams on. He watched his older brother play football over the years and decided one day, the bands were not for him; he wanted to play football. Well, he wasn't fooling me. I knew what that was all about, "the girls." So, I had to endure the pain of sitting in the football stand some days, cold, rainy, and too hot.

Game after game, watching this child with no talent whatsoever, just so the girls and his mother could see him on the field. I remember one game; I was sitting in the stands reading a book that I became accustomed to bringing regularly. The crowd was going wild, and suddenly, I heard, "TOUCH DOWN, #34 LaMar Davis." I quickly looked! Wow! Sadly, I missed the whole play. He was so excited! I became the actress of the decade and played along because there was no way I could tell him his mother had missed his only touchdown.

LaMar loved to cook. His favorite was breakfast, homemade waffles. Entertainment became his passion. He loved making people laugh and looking out for his friends. He wore this custom-made mask to masquerade happiness. He created a way to keep the world around him smiling to ease the pain of sadness hidden inside.

Looking back, I recall one of his close friends sharing a story with me at his viewing, she went on to show gratitude for his willingness to help her daughter; he made himself available no matter the consequence. LaMar knew it was against house rules to be out of the house at that time of the morning, but he risked getting in trouble to help his friend. She was grateful for his caring heart and made him a huge breakfast. This was my first time hearing the reason behind the punishment LaMar got for breaking curfew that morning. He said, "Mom, I needed to help a friend."

LaMar had masked his illness as long as he could until the weight became too heavy to carry alone. He admitted that he was struggling with alcohol abuse, which led to a six-month, inpatient, all-male drug and alcohol rehabilitation program. He was not only the youngest but also the only one who didn't have a drug addiction.

The first few weeks were tough, and he didn't want to be

there. All the men thought he was a smart aleck. This feeling of being an outsider shortly ran its course. He won the respect of the older men and the hearts of the older women who helped with the program. Once, he humbled himself and remembered the talk we once had when he was just a tiny boy about how and when to correct adults. He started communicating on a level that didn't intimidate his peers, and he soon realized many of the men never learned how to read or write. LaMar made it his mission to help those who wanted to learn. He looked forward to completing the program, but he enjoyed the feeling of being helpful and making people laugh.

The light brown stripe disappeared from the center of LaMar's face, but the light that shined beneath never disappeared.

At the rising of the sun and as the dawn begins, I remember your light. You have shone dramatically in this life and have lit up my dark days with the memory of your smile. I have learned to look for you as the sun gently kisses my heart, and as the moon crosses the sky, you will always be the light of my life.

Through moments of stillness, a gentle breeze overtakes me, and the chimes hanging beyond my window begin to sing. I hear you, feel you, and breathe you as you take time to comfort me.

You are and will always be my beautiful, loving, funny morning joy. I can still smell the waffles you loved so much and taste the happiness I can no longer see. You are my never-ending beacon of light, ever-illuminating and forever bright.

Sifting through the leaves of autumn and basking in the coolness of spring, I often look to the skies, and my heart sings. No particular tune, but you are my melody. In the rhythm of your heart, as it connects with mine, we are the music that resonates in my mind.

There is no sense of responsibility as we are free to dance; we move about the earth, holding love in our hands. A certain peculiarity is widely misunderstood. With our consumption of phenomenal and a splash of extraordinary, our bond is secure. You are everlasting from the beginning.

# CHAPTER 6

# Triggers

# BREAKING

## THE STIGMA

## Myth #6

*There's no way to prevent a mental health condition from developing.*

Implementing protective measures to minimize risk factors helps. Some things are unavoidable like genetics and predisposition to an illness. But managing those can prevent larger issues from occurring. Mitigating factors that lead to trauma and environmental challenges can also prevent problems.

www.etactics.com

I just lost my son, and now I'm losing my mind. What is happening to me? No one talks about how different events, or someone's appearance, can initiate a reaction so heartfelt that it causes you to sob out of control—leaving you drained and missing the touch and even the scent of your loved one.

My girlfriend and I decided to attend a local concert one evening, and I was so excited because this band was one of my favorite groups. The artist had terrific vocals, and the band was smoking hot! I was on my feet dancing and having a good old time when I spotted the drummer, and to my surprise, he looked amazingly like my son, LaMar. In a flash, tears began to roll down my face, then a multitude of tears as though someone opened the floodgates. The horrifying part was that I could not control this emotion. I was grateful the music was so loud that no one could hear me, not even my friend. I had taken my seat when she noticed something was not right. She asked in a concerned tone, "What's wrong? Are you alright?" I managed to explain the drummer looked like LaMar. The tears slowly halted, and I had the urge to find the drummer.

I desperately needed to wrap my arms around my son. As I was exiting the concert, from a distance, I spotted the band's crew standing near an elevator, waiting to get in. I rushed as fast as I could through the herd of people. I must at least touch his arm. Sad to say, by the time I reached the area, the elevator doors were closing. My feelings were hurt, yet my heart was filled with joy for a moment when I saw my baby. Don't be afraid of these moments; embrace and enjoy the memories of your loved one. I promise you are not losing your mind.

I was shopping one day, in Home Depot of all places, and I walked past a young man whose stature fit my son's. He had the same skin tone, height, and smile. Suddenly, I had an overwhelming desire to hold my baby in my arms. I paced around the garden area several times, trying to work up the nerves to approach this person. How could I do it without looking like a mad person? All I knew then was I couldn't let this man leave the store. Finally, I stopped him. I will never forget how scared I was because I had no clue what I would say or how to say it.

Excuse me, sir, I promise I'm not crazy. My son committed suicide two years ago, and you greatly favor him. I began to cry. I want to ask you if I could have a hug. He replied, "Oh yes, ma'am," he wrapped his arms around me and held me tight for a few seconds, which seemed like an eternity. For a short while, I relived every time LaMar saw me, he would give me a huge hug and kiss me on the lips. I couldn't help but give God the glory because losing a child leaves you with holes in your heart and loneliness. This was an exceptional day; my tattered void was filled with love.

One year passed, and I hadn't had a single breakdown. I thought, what's wrong with me? As a cosmetologist, I have been a shoulder, a listening ear for over 30 years. I have experienced dealing with grief through the blessings of women who sit in my chair. Some have lost children, and homes endured their health crises, and I had never broken down or lost my calm. I thought I would have expressed a multitude of emotions from the loss of my son, but I managed to remain exempt. What was wrong with me?

One of my absolute best friends lost his son the year after LaMar's death. There was no second thought to show up for support. Who but I understood what he and his wife were going through? I hadn't seen this child in a few years, and now he's lying peacefully in the foyer of my church. As everyone came to view, I remember thinking, wow, you're doing good.

After viewing, I found a seat a few rows from the front. As the funeral directors began to usher the young man in, it felt as if a cloud was covering my body. I knew something was happening that I couldn't explain. In an instant, I was sitting at my son's funeral. I had to get out, but I couldn't move.

What was I going to do? I was about to lose it completely. A voice inside said, "Look to your right." The church was filled with people who adored this young man, but I only saw my pastor. I knew if I could reach him, I would be okay. I cannot tell you how I made it to the other side, but as soon as I reached my pastor, I couldn't stop crying. God gave him the right words to comfort me. I was finally freed from my will to uphold a pillar of strength for others to grieve my son.

God never leaves those who genuinely put their trust in him. LaMar was our passionate child; he never let a holiday, birthday, or Mother's Day pass without presenting a gift. Most of the time, it was something he created himself. It didn't surprise me when I felt the urge to go out and buy myself something special shortly after his death. I decided to purchase a beautiful pair of heart-shaped diamond stud earrings. They were gorgeous! I didn't shop sparingly; they were the most I'd ever spent on a piece of jewelry. I didn't care; this was for my son.

One day, I was getting ready for an event and wanted to wear my beautiful studs, but they were gone. I looked everywhere, and a sense of panic set in. They were gone. An overwhelming feeling of broken- heartedness consumed me like I was entangled in a blanket of pain. My heart was racing, and I fell to my knees; I knew I was having a heart attack. I cried out to God for His help, and it was as if I couldn't hear myself through the beating of my heart. I cried out,

"Lord, please help me"! At that moment, the anxiety began to exit my body. God had wrapped his arms of comfort around me.

Through the comfort and peace found in the gentle hand of God, I remembered I placed my beautifully shaped diamond earrings in a safe place. Later, I found my heart again. My earrings were safe, and my heart was secure.

It's been eleven years, and I still have moments when someone or something will remind me of the precious memories forever carved into my very soul. There will continue to be days when grief triggers an overwhelming cloud of *loneliness*. Don't try to fight it or resist it; embrace the moment. It will soon pass. It amazes me that a simple sound of a simple melody of a simple song can bring me back to a moment in time.

I was home alone one day listening to satellite radio, and one of the songs used on LaMar's memorial video came on. It sent me flying down memory lane; all the happy times flooded my mind. For some reason, I thought pulling out the DVD and watching it was a great idea. I hadn't watched it in quite some time. This will surely be okay, right... NOT. I was paralyzed for what seemed like forever. I managed to grab the urn my son's remains are housed in and open the top. I was crying uncontrollably, yet I had to be near my child. I cradled a small hand full of what felt like sand and placed him on my chest. As I replayed the video, I began to rock as though my infant child was lying atop my bosom. Little did I know God was watching over me. At the end of the video, I got up, cleaned myself up, and left the house. Grief was trying to swallow me whole. God gave me the strength to visit the moment, feel my son, and continue my life.

I cherish the nuances and quirky places in time as they have their set assignments. I am open to the shelter found in the awakening of its clock. Every second is accounted for and may never have its opportunity to pass again.

Though we falter, fail, and sin, our God is mighty; in our weaknesses, He stands us up again. It is an unprecedented feat we have faced, yet we are saved through His grace. What an unexplainable feeling to actively seek His face!

In our time of uncertainty, hurt, and fear, our hope is in God; on Him, we can depend. Never-failing, all- powerful Father, Son, and Friend. Thank you, Lord, for allowing me to hold my son again.

# CHAPTER 7

## In The Midst Of The Storm

# BREAKING
## THE STIGMA

# *Myth #7*

*Therapy and getting help is a waste of time.*

Out of around 59 million people who received mental health treatment in two years, around 80% found it effective. The average person who receives psychotherapy is better off than 79% of those who don't receive treatment.

" "

www.etactics.com

Once you lose a loved one, emotions set in almost immediately. A dark cloud roars in like a monster coming to devour you whole, leaving you with an enormous hole filled with sadness, doubt, disbelief, guilt, and many other emotions. Everyone's story is different, and grief comes in many forms and stages.

As a parent, you are programmed to do all the routine things that come with raising a child. We are responsible for providing food, clothing, shelter, and education, not to mention the things they want. As I looked at my son's eternally resting body, I began to ask questions. I started to experience an emotion that I could not explain. Why didn't you let me help you? You left before becoming the man I knew you would be one day. You had that beautiful, expensive smile. I just sent your semester payment to the University; you were doing well. All my hopes and dreams for you are gone. He didn't need me anymore; I was no longer needed as a mother to my LaMar. On the outside, I appeared strong, but secretly, inside, I was having all these visions. Anger had crept its ugly head into my space as I grieved the loss of my son. I was not ready for my son to be gone forever.

I was so mad that my baby was gone, I could scream! I bottled up all my anger and felt like I would implode! From the inside out, I could feel my blood boiling, and the heat from its rage melted my heart. I was lost, and I could not find myself. I pretended to be the warrior woman who could withstand anything; all the while, I was unrecognizable. Who had I become? Where had I gone? A mystical place of the unknown is where I chose to reside. Or did I? I was a confused, angry, lost soul and couldn't find any sense of peace. My beautiful boy was gone.

I remembered his words from the letter. "This is a personal choice that I have made for myself." I had to smile because this is precisely the young man I raised him to be. As time passed, I began to channel that energy into the happy moments we had shared. The long talks we shared, which I always had to prepare myself for because if you asked, he would overly tell you the truth. All the times he beat me playing a game of pool, the hugs and kisses, the laughter, and all the special holidays. And, just like that, no more anger.

Every year for four years, despite what I knew, I believed my son would walk through the front door at any given time. I secretly waited every day. I could not shake the feeling or accept the reality that I would never see my son again. I didn't understand; I physically saw him lying dead, yet I still waited for him. I prayed every day, please, Lord, help me. I was in denial, and that response to my loss held me captive for four years. Finally, at the end of the fourth year, it was as if a dark cloud was lifted from my very being. I can't explain it. God must have heard my prayers, and He answered them. An illuminating presence of joy and a calming peace entered my soul. I fell to my knees and wept. At that very moment, the truth set in, and my youngest child was gone forever. I would never physically touch, feel, smell, get mad, or hug him again in this lifetime. Yet, I had been gifted twenty-five years of precious memories housed indefinitely in my heart.

Grief will manifest itself in many forms. Sadness is the most common. I was sad the child who showed up every holiday, birthday, and Mother's Day with a big smile chose not to show up anymore. Anger is one of the most confusing feelings because if you are not careful, blame is directed toward another person. I didn't want to be around anyone. Guilt will have you questioning yourself. Could I have done more? The instant that officer told me my son had committed suicide, my body was shocked. Of course, I would experience loneliness. My child was not missing; he was gone forever. Other emotions like fatigue, helplessness, yearning, anticipation, relief, and numbness can occur. The most important lesson is that these are all normal grief reactions. When I focused on the good times we shared along the way, those moments of grief became smaller and smaller.

An older woman who had lost her daughter once told me, "Whenever you start to miss your child, you find yourself a corner and cry out to the Lord, Thank You." I listened, but how could saying "thank you" to God ease this intense pain? I hated the pain, so if expressing to God how grateful I was for giving me LaMar, even for such a short time, somehow stopped the hurt, I had to try it. So, at the start of every episode, I would go into my prayer closet and begin thanking Him for loving me so much that He trusted me with His child for twenty-five years. Most importantly, I never asked why this happened to me or why He chose to take my son away. I genuinely believe that was my saving grace. God began to fill that empty hole, once occupied with loneliness and filled it with peace and great people who just wanted to love me.

The biggest lesson I learned through this experience was that it's not about me. LaMar's journey with mental illness was something he alone had lived through. I cannot imagine what his world looked like if only we could walk in another's shoes or take away someone's pain. His pain, as awful as it seemed, has become my purpose.

To fulfill the plan for my pain, I had to endure. I had to be overcome by the blood of the lamb. LaMar was my lamb, and I never wanted to see the sacrifice or experience the significant loss of my blessing. Through his turmoil, there was a testimony hidden in the tumultuous unrest. A mind so beautiful, it couldn't stay in this land but gifted us with a blueprint to a blooming of many buds. As his garden grows from the seeds that have been planted, I am reminded of the rain.

With our youthful dance and our unequivocal parade, as we march through the trenches of this victorious battle, we have won the keys to our future by acknowledging the past that shapes our today to form our tomorrows. Although our many hopes for the future are not promised, we are pleased with our new and surrounded by all the nuances that have aided in our thought processes to become who we are in this exact moment, not taken for granted, but grateful for its joys and subject to its pain. We are here. We are today.

# CHAPTER 8

# God's Plan

# BREAKING

## THE STIGMA

## *Myth #8*

*I can handle my problems on my own.*

32% of people not in therapy think that they can handle their problems on their own. This is partly because 30% of them think that their problems aren't "big enough." There are some self-care steps that people can take to manage symptoms. But in most cases, mental illness won't get better without any professional care.

I've never questioned God why my son had to leave me; however, I have said more than once, "God has a sense of humor." I just funeralized my son, and you want me to go to mortuary school?

During my journey in mortuary school, I did question myself. Why would I listen to the voice inside that asked me to complete such a difficult task? My faith was so strong when the voice of God so vividly said, "Go learn how to help others have a better experience." I just went and signed up. I didn't think twice about it, and I never even took the time to research the program or its packages. I will never forget the day I received the school's curriculum. I was standing at the desk in the front office, and tears began to run down my face. At that moment, I thought, what did I get myself into? A slew of thoughts raced through my head—I hadn't been to school in thirty years. I can't do this. I have already paid these people my money. This is too much. I read too slowly. The more I read, the more anxiety began to drown me. I was overwhelmed.

How hard can it be? You go learn how to preserve and prepare a loved one for their viewing. Wow, was I ever wrong! I have said and will say, even to this day, that experience was the second hardest thing (besides burying my son) I have ever done. Right in the middle of my meltdown, a distinguished, well- groomed older gentleman approached me and introduced himself as one of the instructors. He put his hand on my shoulder and said, "Don't you worry; you will do just fine." he also assured me that I was not the only forty-plus-year-old in the class. Boy, was he right. Kids were coming right from high school to middle age to seniors. I felt right at home.

When I entered that school mentally, I was not as prepared as I thought. There was still an emptiness inside of me, like a gigantic hole. I had not truly faced the grieving part of losing LaMar. I thought keeping busy would cure the pain buried deep inside. Through this journey, God had a plan. I, of course, had no clue what that plan looked like; I was willing to trust God had my back.

I was exiting the school office when a young lady approached me, unaware she was in the office at the same time, and overheard me talking to the instructor. She said to me, "I will help you."

That same year, I opened a 2700 sq. ft beauty salon as the owner, manager, and full-time hairstylist. How on earth was I going to manage to go to school full-time? One of my stylists watched me struggle with the timing and said, "Do not worry about your clientele; I will help you."

The manifestation of God's plan was becoming a reality. All I had to do was trust. He had already prepared the path to welcome me with open arms. Once I got settled into school, my faith was tested. I had never met anyone who did not believe in God; however, not one but many young people there professed to be atheists. As I watched and listened to their stories, many were hurting inside, sad, and depressed. Dismissed in society as troubled, with no direction, or crazy. Since many of them were close to my son's age and as a mother, I could relate to their pain. To my surprise, I found it amazingly comfortable to listen and to love every one of them. As I boldly shared my son's story of his struggles and ultimate decision to commit suicide, the more I began to gain their trust. Before I knew it, I became the mother to many and was voted in as Chaplain of the class of 2011.

I had a genuine peace that drew these young adults to my heart. Before long, that massive hole that once harbored loneliness and demise began to be filled with love and friendships. I had one remaining son alive, and now I had multiple sons and daughters. God was restoring the children and healing me at the same time. I am so grateful that I had the courage to open my mouth and share my story and the empathy to love someone else just because.

Like so many, I did not feel like I needed additional help or counseling after my son's death. I just threw myself into my work non-stop. I thought if I stayed busy, I did not have the time to think about never seeing my son again. One day, while in class studying how to help others understand and work through the grief process, something happened; It was as if the words jumped off the page onto my body. My eyes watered, and I remember thinking, "Wow, this is me." I was not aware my non-stop work was placing a mask over my grief to numb my pain. I realized sharing my testimony, crying out loud, feeling lonely, and talking with a counselor are all part of healing. Now, when grief knocks on my door, I no longer hide. I open the door and experience the moment. Then I get up and gently close the door. What I know for sure is that grief will swallow you and try to hold you captive if you do not understand the power within.

During this period, I was very vulnerable and naïve in many ways. I trusted all with whom I shared my story. I so desperately wanted to help others navigate their loss that I left my heart unguarded to those whose intent was not always favorable. Keep your faith; this season will not last long. God has a way of revealing the darkness. Yet, I remember saying, "God, you have a sense of humor." Partly because the path was not yet clear.

Shortly after school, I was given the opportunity to co-own a funeral home. I was delighted to have the chance to share the gift God had given me. While in school, I discovered God had given me the gift of restorative art. After experiencing the devastation of the person who embalmed my son's body, my passion became caring for the deceased. I believe God heard my cry. I wanted no other mother or father to experience nothing but peace on this journey. Recreating natural form and color is a natural talent I will always treasure...the inner joy I get when I see the face of someone who must face the fear of seeing their loved one physically for the last time. Creating a sense of peace and comfort is what they see. It exudes a reassurance that their son, daughter, sister, or brother is with God. The healing begins at that point. I want people to see and feel I care.

Right away, God sent a mother whose son committed suicide. He was my son's age, skin tone, body frame, and the same wound. I remember looking up and saying, "God, you got some sense of humor"! I did not know if I could do it. Once I met the mother, unaware, I immediately went into protective mode. Sharing my story assured her I understood where she was right then. I wanted her to know I would take great care of her baby.

Once I received her son, he spiritually became my child. I wept as I washed his face and combed his hair. My whole frame of mind was on my experience. I would not let that mother come close to feeling the anger I was left to bear.

With God's help, I was going to restore him to look like his natural self, as though he was just asleep, and this mother could begin her journey of healing.

With my hand in her hand and my arm around her shoulders, I said, it is time to see your child. Even though God had prepared me through mortuary school for this long walk ahead, grief did not care. Tears rained down, for this was a long walk toward forever. I felt the pain of her loss, and I wanted her to know she was not alone. Her tears were once mine, and today, we shared them.

At that moment, God's plan became clear. I looked up, but this time, I said, "Lord, this is not only about the gift you gave me of restorative art, but this is my Ministry."

Would I have accepted this road if I had known the plan God had for me when my LaMar was born? I don't know that my faith would have allowed me to see the blessing in the untimely removal of my son, but I am grateful that God is all-knowing and holds us in the palm of His hands. He has guided me when my heart has blinded me and my mind could not think clearly, and today I am at rest. On the bosom of my Lord, I have cried, and now I can smile again. What a phenomenal gift!

# CHAPTER 9

## Highs & Lows

# BREAKING

## THE STIGMA

## Myth #9

### *Getting help is a sign of weakness.*

47% of Americans think that getting mental health therapy is a sign of weakness. Stigma is one of the biggest reasons why people don't get help, even though many recognize it as a problem. Because of this, it's a sign of strength to get help because you show bravery by going

" "

www.etactics.com

Coping is like putting a sealed top on an open wound that will never heal. Years have passed, and I look back, wondering how I made it. I live each day missing my son, longing for his presence. The first thing I did automatically was throw myself into my work. I filled my days with work; if I was never home, I did not have to feel the pain of missing LaMar.

I remember asking myself, "Why would he do that"? "Why would my baby not want to live anymore"? and "Why would he not let me help him?" Then I remembered his last words, "This has nothing to do with you. This is a personal choice that I have made for myself."

That was his way of assuring me that he would be all right. This made me smile, which gave me peace knowing my son was no longer sad, lonely, or depressed living in a world of constant darkness. This was a good day.

I started writing this book three years ago; during this time, I lost my mother, who was seventy-six years old. I was home when I got the call. I was devastated. A few hours later, I went to work. I allowed my work to imprison my emotions so I did not have to face the ache of emptiness, sorrow, and simply missing my son and mom. Of course, my dad's demise was one year before LaMar's suicide.

It was not until I went to grief counseling that I ever thought I was masking my grief, or, as she put it, "distractions," by disappearing into my work. I had to appear strong, for that is what my child expects of me. Quote, "I know you are a strong person." In silence, I want to scream, "Who told you that?" I am not strong; I want you back with me.

Work was a coping defense mechanism for me. If I stopped working, it would have been like pulling that sealed top off an open wound desperately trying to heal. Honestly, I did not want to feel the pain, I did not want to feel the loneliness, and I did not want to face the reality that I would never see my son again. Everyone deals with grief in their own way, if you choose to deal with it at all.

Some forms of happiness can be found by holding your head up, putting a smile on your face, and moving forward. People around me would say, "You are so strong," and they appear genuine. Here is the truth: You must be careful and watchful of the people you allow in your space during this time. Be intentional with whom you even share your story. Most are genuine with their concerns for you and indeed mean what they say, "Call me if you need anything." Whether you do or not, they are standing by waiting on your call, or they might show up in texts, phone calls, and even in person.

It can get hushed at times, and those gestures made me smile. However, I never called in fear of that dreaded sound of silence once the exchange of pleasantries was met. It is as if LaMar committing suicide was some form of taboo. No surprise. Generally, we do not wish to talk about death. This was my child; I want someone to listen.

What I did not expect was to see people watching and listening to my stories for their gain. I couldn't see them as predators because they wore masks to disguise themselves as friends, lovers, and kind Christians. I was naïve.

Predators sit back, watch your every move, and listen to your most vulnerable thoughts about your loved ones as though they care. Once that happens, you have permitted them to enter your space. Now, they prepare to pounce and will attempt to destroy your peace. Stay strong; predators do not stay around long. Their lust for greed keeps them from being stagnant, and they must feed their desire. The poorly yet inviting costume created to lure you into their den will quickly fade as they devour every part of you; you are the prey. It's funny how this can occur all in the name of love. This was not a good day.

This level of trust can either be rewarding or damaging to your mental state. When you are numb inside and desperate to have that void be made whole again, you welcome any remnant of kindness. To have it ripped away just when the illusion of healing begins to form well, it feels like the tempered scales of loneliness begin to bleed—invaded by a tsunami of grief again.

I found myself reminiscing and remembering the mother's words, "Go into your private space and cry loudly unto the Lord," as I was obedient to her wisdom, the Lord appeared and granted a new peace. This was a good day.

Though I have had a series of emotions and a whirlwind of factual and alternative truths, I lean on the Lord. My heart has been shaken, and my mind has fought beyond the weakness of guilt. Where I am weak, the Lord has been faithful and kept me near Him. Yes, LaMar, I am strong.

# CHAPTER 10

# A New Day

# BREAKING

## THE STIGMA

# Myth #10

*People with mental illness are more violent.*

It's a common misconception that people with mental illness are more aggressive or have violent tendencies. In developed countries, 7-8% of people believe that to be true. In developing countries, 15-16% of people agree with this misconception, too. But people with mental illness are more likely to harm themselves than others.

My son assumed I and the world would automatically say or think crazy thoughts on why he killed himself. He said, "This has nothing to do with you, or a girl, or drugs, or whatever crazy stupid thing you and everyone else have already assumed." Again, we are conditioned to throw mental illness "under the bus" by not calling the illness by the correct name. The word "crazy" has become the norm when we talk about someone experiencing symptoms of anxiety, bipolar depression, PTSD, or any of the many disorders.

I, myself, was guilty of many years of saying the word "crazy." During the period before my son was clinically diagnosed, he was acting erratic. He had no regard for the law. Drinking and driving, grades dropping, not remembering where he left his car for weeks, and I would say, "Why are you acting so crazy?" The more I used the word "crazy," the more his actions seemed "crazy."

It was not until I began to pay closer attention to his behavior and patterns. I had become "Mother Snooper." I was snooping around without my son noticing. Then, I started asking questions, which led us to get medical attention. I learned my sweet, intelligent child was not "crazy," and I should never use that word again.

LaMar had been living with a chemical imbalance in his brain, and he had been managing it the best he could. The only way for him to feel "normal" was to drink alcohol and use street drugs.

I realized that for my son to trust this new diagnosis, I had to change how I viewed his behavior and call it by its correct name. When people feel no one sees them or their problem because we constantly use the term "crazy," they will not have the desire or the courage to receive or ask for help. The typical response is, "Why should I? You think I'm crazy anyway!" Or something to that effect.

After completing a six-month in-house alcohol and drug recovery program, LaMar returned to the University with talks of changing his major to Psychology. He hoped to help the many kids who struggle with the underdiagnosed diseases that plague their brains. He wanted them to understand they could live everyday lives and be productive, happy members of the mainstream community. Consistently reiterating the need to know they were not "crazy."

The struggle became exhausting for LaMar, and he consciously decided to end the pain. He said, "I'm just tired of fighting so hard to feel what everybody feels normally. I did this for me." He also said, "But my whole life, I experienced pockets of happiness while living the vast majority of my life feeling terrible inside."

I had no choice but to dry my tears, trust my faith, and attempt to move forward. I genuinely miss my son, but no way did I want him to return to live in such darkness. I know he is with my heavenly Father, and he hurts no more.

What I hold dear to my existence is that my God trusted me to love and cherish His son for twenty- five years. How precious am I to Him that He chose me?

Although I will never fully understand the magnitude of suffering my son endured, I am comforted in knowing that he gave me the blueprint for recognizing, treating, and coping with mental illness. No, he was not “crazy” because Crazy Has A Name.

My Dearest LaMar,

Thank you for allowing me to be your mother and for loving me beyond your resting place. You are constant, and there is a stillness in your mind; you are at peace.

I am grateful for your gratitude and adorned with the beauty of your mind. As you soar among the clouds and drift in the sky, you leave me with fond memories, and you have proven yourself to be an inspiration to those who could not find the words to speak. You spoke on their behalf. You have helped us all to see that we are not all the same, but we are uniquely crafted and cannot be replicated. Our normal is what we make it, and we don't have to fit in.

We are set apart, and you have allowed us to see inside the mind of a genius longing to be free.

Fly.

With all my love,
Mom

## CHAPTER 11

# I Must Write

In 2009, on February 19th, LaMar made a personal choice to end his life. Quote, "I did this for me," "I'm just tired of fighting so hard to feel what everybody feels normally."

But, before saying goodbye, LaMar wanted to share a piece of his beautiful mind through journaling; some have even described them as a "literary masterpiece."

LaMar hoped his writing would inspire change for the better in those lives he touched.

I must write, I don't know why; but I must, one day
I may compose a literary master piece. Maybe that
masterpiece will simply be a collection of my writings
over the course of my life found in a bibliographical
text of my life. One day I hope to inspire those
lifes that I touch, wheather that be through spoken
or written word. I hope to one day be seen as
monumental figure in this world, changing lifes
4 the better, on the terms that that individual sets. I'm
like Jesus in the sense that I see a wicked $ corrupt
system controling a land full of lost $ misguided souls.
One day my time will come, I will show all the world
everything they need to see and tell them everything
they need to hear, but I will speak nothing of what
"THEY" want to hear, reveal nothing that "THEY"
want uncovered. The truth, @ least a possible version
of it. I will do all that I can to bring forth a future
that is the ultimate goal of every person,
but is seen only as a fantasy, a pipe dream
an illusion. There is nothing stopping me from being all
that I strive to be, so therefore my greatest opstical
is myself. @ least that is the 1st real challenge in a
series of challenges that is already laid before me:
Hatred, intolerance, racism, bigotry, closed-mindedness,
fear, comfort, greed, deseption. Those are my obstacles,
Those are my challenges, those are my enemies.

I am prepared to die @ anytime. That statement should not be misconstrued, I don't want to die @ least not right now, or even soon for that matter. But I do not fear death. It is a considerable outcome in all that I do, but dying to me would one amazing adventure, which I would be happy to embark on @ any moment.

I just can't shake the feeling that something is not right in this world. I look around as if through eyes that have seen it all b4. As if through eyes that have been exposed to this world of lies, $ deceit. $ bull...., $ greed, hate, jealousy. All though I may or may not have been exposed to those things and then some, I feel as if none of that is new, in fact, that's why I hate the news the most, it reports on the same thing day in $ day out violence, poverty, death, $ destruction. I've seen it, but I haven't seen it I know it, but I don't KNOW it. It is as though I have been here before, $ I'm sick of it. Its either that or there is a piece of my soul that rembers being in a place where all was right in the world. Perhaps all the destain & distgust that I harbor towards this world is a result of a part of me that can not let go of a better life that I once knew. Or Perhaps a connection that I have with the spiritual world allows me to Know what bliss feels like & my physical self responds with a negative feeling toward everything here in this imperfect world.

GLoDo

I know I've talked on this b4, @ some point or not, who cares NEEK wayz, "I want to die" And I want to explain that because it is a little out of context when it stands alone I must to die not for selfish or stupid reasons. I don't want to hang myself or OD on Advil or something equally as stupid I don't always necessarily enjoy living, mostly for the simple fact that I can't find too much to be happy for or about, or things that REALLY make me happy. I look at the world that I live in & can't help but feel that there's a better place, that all is not right in this world & somewhere, perhaps a place I've been b4, perhaps not, but a place none the less exist. A place away from all the negativity that I can't help but focus on that exist and is exposed to us human beings. whether I've experienced it or not, I feel all kinds of pain, the news upsets my stomach, I can't stand to watch it. The news most disgustes (sp) me.

TV programing makes me feel similar. Theres too much something in this world, off the top of my head no I word can describe it or do it justice. Evil is not enough although it would be something on the lines of that.

No real purpose or destination is in mind. I simply must write. The pen must move & the ink must flow. Y? Y Sometimes I want to stop asking. I am beginning to realize that I don't have the answers for the questions I can't ask. Y There is a void that I can not fill, constantly calling out to me from the darkness I hear ∴ something, however its not clear. I can not understand what the voice is saying, but I hear it. Bellowing at from the depths of deep dark chasm in my soul, beckoning to be filled, but w/ what? Y can't I understand, Y won't the answers come? where are they? DO I have the answers? My mothers suggestion to talk to a Doc. is starting to sound more & more tempting. Yet I am notoriously stubburn, & stupid, am I ready to give up on... me.

been apart of the miracle that we as humans call life. a reason for existing would ultimatly involve the existance of another for example, you can say grass exist for sects to eat, & those insects exist in order to pollenate flowers & other plants, or be eaten by another organism, and so on & so forth. Life on this planet exist as a system, on top of a system, on top of a system... One part works b/c of another and exist to help aid the functions of another part of life, creating a balance, "The Circle of Life"

---

All life stems from the same root, originates from the same source, "God" to some, "Allah" or what have u others simply refer to this life giving force as "life", God is life, & life is God those 2 words are (@ least I have come to believe that) interchangable where you say "God" replace w/ "life" & you can see how the meaning may change, but the basic underline principal my still remain. "In the beginning "God" created the heavens & earth" / "In the beginning "life" created the heavens & earth" I hate the way ppl think that "God" only favors a certain few, his "chosen people". Ever since I was a child

I've heard about groups of people, all so much very diffrent,
but w/ one overbearing similarity; they all believe tht they
are "God's" only blessed ppl, that God favors them over all
others for whatever reason. Jews, Christans, Black ppl, white ppl,
Asians, muslims, you name it. If only 1 of those groups
of peoples is truely Gods chosen few, then there are a
whole, whole, whole bunch of people doomed to damnation.
Why would God do that? why would God create all
these diffrent people if He only realy liked just the one
group? Why would God create an infinate number of
stars & only have life on one planet that orbits 1 of
these countless number of stars? People are selfish &
greedy by nature, thus their views on God & religion must
also reflect that selfishness, jealousy, & greed. Man wants
therefore "God" must want. Man needs, therefore God must
need, right? WRONG for so long has God been viewed
as a supersized version of man, only perfect & all powerful,
a creator seperate from His creations This view leaves God
subseptable to basic human emotions & feelings. Humans like
to own things, even other people, so it would only make sense
that God not only likes to own things, but also needs them
like humans. Why would the creater of all things past, present,
& future need any one thing from anybody for any reason.
Why did Jesus Christ die so that we could get into heaven?
If God <u>wanted</u> His people to be able to have salvation &
everlasting life in heaven, why would He feel the <u>need</u>

to send "His only begotten Son" to DIE? Can "God" not speak the words or think the thoughts neccessary to save His people w/out having to sacrafice "His only begotten Son"! There is nothing that "God" wants because He has everything. There is nothing "God" needs because He is everything. There is nothing "God" He is perfection, He is all that there is. So why is it that any of my insignificant actions may "hurt" "God" or "displease" or "anger" "God". If something that I'm doing pisses God off so much, why doesn't He kill me, or just watch somebody else?" How is it that "God" a symbol of love, passion, & forgiveness be the meanist, badest S.O.B. @ the same time. Eternal bliss or everlasting damnation, all issued out to souls for following certain rules & guidelines that God has issued to His chosen people. These are not the actions of a true all loving, mercyful God. Why create a planet full of people but only like a certain few?

I, First of all am hesitant to call myself a "man". The preconceived
notion of what a "man" is for the most part does not go along very
concordantly w/ what I would describe myself as being. But a
man I am none the less. I am a man of some knowledge,
some wisdom, & an understanding nature that I myself do not
fully comprehend. There is much of myself, my life, & this
world that to this point I have questioned. I have focused
so long on all that I consider to be bull...., that I have
let my life become that. For too long have I shed light
on to darkness, & in doing so I have wandered into that
darkness & let my light be ingulfed by it, & extinguish
it. For too long have I stumbled about in the dark, lost
& unsure. But alas I have felt it. The spark that will
relight the darkness & make it no more. It is as if
I suddenly remembered that I had the clapper, and all
I had to do to make the dark go away was clap.
So I clapped & clapped & clapped but still no light.
Now I know that when I clap my hands the light should
come on & the darkness lifted, but there was nothing, still
dark. But there's something funny about being in the dark, once
you're there, you notice that there is no difference btwn the
dark, & the dark behind your eyes. And it was @ this
moment that I realized that there was no darkness to begin
w/ All the troubles, & trials that I so called "suffered"
from in the darkness where only so because I made them so.
Because the darkness that I was in was w/ me all the
time, I simply closed my eyes & forgot how to open them.
Now w/ my eyes open & well rested I see my light,
shining brite, never gone, never extinguished, just out of sight.

There are times when uncertainty and doubt will plague your mind to the brink of insanity. Ultimatly that feeling must be overcame lest that nature of the insane take hold & drive you to do things that later may be regretable. Often times I find, no, better yet found, myself @ this point, tetering @ the edge of darkness, peering over the edge into the blk abyss of darkness that threatend to swallow me up whole w/out remorse if my life were to end, w/ my limted knowledge, I could only speculate & assume my fate from that point toward There are tons & tons of ppl who claim to have the answer, the key to salvation that will lead you to the place where suffering is but a memory. I'm sorry but that place is called the relm of the dead in which all suffering known to human beings ceases to exist, literaly, & for now I say this b/c suffering is a result of mans own flawed nature. No man was braght here to suffer. No one was or is nor will be here on this planet, "destined" to suffer. Life is what you make it. For too long have I sought deliverance from painly way of death. Yes this is the ultimate conclusion to all that lives as we know it, but that word, "death", its meaning applies only to those who know of that word & its meaning

I do not know how where, or when my end will come I do not fear that day, I embrace it. I don't look forward to it. Not anymore. There was a time not long ago when death was more prevelent in my mind than any other thought or emotion. Now I can honestly say my thoughts are pro-life. This does not mean that the underline cause of my bleak outlook $ depressed state has been Identified. Some times I have "flashbacks" or better yet minor relapses, but most of the time I dismiss it b4 I dwell on it too long. Which has proven to be effective. Unexplained, sometimes extreme mood swings still run ramped. Irritability, most often is what mood I flash to. So bad that everything/everyone gets on my nerves. It's @ those times where solitude or weed seems to work best. Anything to settle my mind. Bi-Polar. Theres a good possibility but I don't know enough about it or the symptoms. But I'll look further into it. No matter the (diagnosous)? I will prevail $ conquer that obstacle like all others that fell b4 me in my life. Thank you God for the strength courage $ fortitude to handle all these things that I perceive to be problems. I know that You have a plan 4 me $ together we will change the world make it a better place to live. →

The Kingdom of God that Jesus spoke of, The Kingdom the
exist in each of our hearts will be realized & I might have
an important role to play in this. Its hard however to bridge
the gap btwn all races, religions, &/or beliefs. For the most part
its against the cardinal rules of religions to question the faith
& its foundation. But I believe that its a mistake to close
the door on the issues & questions & contradictions in the
docturines b/c how else can we improve the state of the world
if we fail to improve the bases of the avg. human life. Maybe
the reason we can't, rather have yet to see peace on this earth
is b/c people are so confused. Their god tells them to love
their brothers & neighbors, but to f... all others, except
you may try to convert them but if that fails, f... 'em!
That's like giving people a license to judge & be an a.-hole.
Why not preach acceptance of the different believes. B/c
Then ppl begin to exchange ideas in a positive light, comparing &
contrasting. Finding the answers to the questions that plague
all groups of ppl on the globe. Find the tie that binds, the
universal constants that traced the pages of the holy texts
of the world. With all the stars in the sky, you would have to be
a fool to think our sun is the only one that has planets w/ life
on them that orbit it. And with all the ppl on this
world & all the religions that exist, you wouldn't be a fool, but
a little ignorant to say that only 1 of them got it right &
once again everybody else is f... ed.

A moment spent w/ nothing to do. So I pick up the pen. But to what end? For what purpose? That is a question that we've asked many times b4. But what then of the answer? Have we yet to discover the heart that lies w/in? But of course! If I had the answer there'd be no question at least not that one. There always has been & always will be questions. But only 1 question that a man asks himself in life truly matters. Who am I? What am I here for? Does it matter? Why is it that so many ppl have to ask this question? Screw that; why is it that I have to ask this question? I have yet to solidify an identity for myself. I live, I have a life & I do "stuff" but who am I really? What am I really? What is a man really? I looked into my eyes this morning. Not just "looked" into my eyes, but seriously peered into my eyes for only a second. You know what I felt, what I saw. Fear. I couldn't look but for a second b4 an eerie feeling came over me. I got scared seriously, & had to look away! What is that about? Is that what's inside my heart & soul? Fear? Is that what ppl see when they look into my eyes?

---

Without my father to raise me I can't help but wonder what kind of effect that has had on me & my psyche? What emotional & psychological scars I have b/c of that. I'm not sure I even know how to be a man, or better yet what it feels like to be a man. Its more then obvious that a man is not what you need be to survive & even reproduce in this world. But it is the men in the world that make differences, make changes, important decisions. Maybe a man is one who chooses to accept the responsibility of what it is to be a man. As flawed as Adam, yet still held to the highest regards in the eyes of God. Strength & courage. Confidence, wisdom. Do those things make a man? Sure men posses these qualities, but to be strong & courages w/out confidence & wisdom to best use your strength & courage then all you have is a big strong kid, unafraid to show & use his strength, but a man he is not. And what of confidence & wisdom Also useless on there own in defining a man. IF all the wisdom in the world resides w/in you & the confidence in yourself that your knowledge is wisdom yet your heart has not the courage to share it for fear of persecution, or the strength to handle that persecution what kind of a true man are you. Sure you may be an "adult" but a man? What do think of a car w/ no engine? Yes it is a car, But what use is it?

I spend much time contemplating many things. My weakness lives in the fact that this process often becomes overwhellming and/or over bearing. Now in order to calm myself or focus my thought I chose/choose to introduce foreign substances into ~~the~~ my body which manipulates my physical being in a manor that brings about a sense of peace or "feels good" which numbs my non-physical self and causes the self that is me (my actual self, the invisible "me" that is) allows me to forget or be content w/ my physical existance. This creates a seperation which most ppl fail to ever acknowledge but 100% of the time express. If you try to separate or draw or see or touch the differention btwn the Earth or the sky, you will find that such a thing is impossible and non-existent. W/ my eyes I see what is percived to be a horizon, a point where land ends and sky begins. But in actuality there is no diffrence btwn land and sky especially when I takes into account the fact that the earth is a mass colaboration of tightly packed light that is literally floating, spinning, and hurling itself through an infinate "space" or void, nothingness No-thingness. Space is a word that has meaning to us as human beings. we label everything give what we observe w/ or eyes a name, a classification, a definiton, in order to create the illusion of control. This gives us a peace of mind that lets us forget the fact that No-thing exist, create a sense of control in a existance that is completly beyond or control. We can give a name to all we see and experience and observe through our senses, but we did not create the core of that which we see. a man made a pen, a man manipulated the raw materials which a pen is comprised of, but that which makes up the pen, the very thing that we are made of existed way b4 any man. Or life is as big a mystery as or percieved notion of God. Emotions are non-physical states of being that is percieved by the bodys consciousness which is connected to the body yet separate all @ once. An emotional response occurs do to the bodys exposer to an outside stimuli. We define or existance based on the environment which we find ourself in. We percieve our ownself by aknowledging the difference btwn "me" and all that is not "me". B/c I was born w/ arms and legs B the consciousness is bond to the body, the human being defines itself as being a creature w/ arms and legs. This is neither true nor false. Yes the self is a creature w/ arms and legs, but that which makes up the creature makes up all that we perceive. The smallest unit that man is able, (to this date) to perceive reveals to our self that all matter is but a specific configuration of tightly bond light energy. focused fields of energy. This energy is pulsating, vibrating, constantly moving and interacting w/ every "thing" that is. Our (human) configuration is what we call the body. We as humans have given a name to all the configurations of energy that we have perceived. But emotions are non-physical. How is it that we can define that which we can not see on a universal level. Chemicals in the brain along w/ electrical signals create those perceived states of consciousness B/c we as humans can recognize this fact, and identify the results of this interaction we can reproduce it, manipulate it, and give it a name. I can describe the sensation that occurs we I put my hand to some "thing" "hot"

My description coillates of the sensation felt by another person, which creates a universal link between 1 person and the next. The problem is that we define or existace based on what the body percieves. The body creates perception, consciousness controls the body, rather it reacts to the body, but they are 2 seperate entities that create a union that we call life. We define some "thing" as living b/c it grows and changes and uses energy. But if that is the case then all that we percieve should be considered alive. B/c we can not experience a existace outside of the body we label all that is not moving "dead" the absence of life. But everything" has an opposite, a side that we can not see, and some times we can see. For every night there is a day. Since we don't know 1st hand what happens to the self it when the body is no longer active, we define it on the bases of what our "living" life experienced. Heaven or hell is given a description that is based on what the body can experience, streets of gold or burning flames. What many fail to realize is that the self does not "feel". the brain interprets sensations and the self is bond to the brain. W/out a physical body or brain, how is it possible to experince a physical sensation? When the self leaves the body, the body remains on the physical plain. The spirit gives definition to the body, the body does not define the spirit. The self percieves or interprets the body and all that happens to it. The self, the inner "I" can not be seen or handled or touched. Heaven and Hell are illusions, make believe places used to control ppl and cause fear in order to force a particular behavior pattern.

The Human Consciousness
The inner "I"
The self

Is a result of, rather,
comes about as a result of
the collective consciousnesses of
each individual part of the body.
The body is a system which is built
on top of, or comprised of individual
Systems and collections of cells, molecules
and atoms, all of which containing its
own identity, its own voice, its own
functions. All of them joined and
working together communicating and
cooperating forms 1 complete unit
1 collective consciousness, ME

But you know it today is yesterday & tommorow is today & while you spent all that energy worried about 2day, yesterday has come and gone and there was so much that could have been done then. Now what r we left w/? More planning 4 2morow. But there are things that need 2 be addressed 2day. Once yesterday has come its 2 late. Something different now needs 2 be done 2day, which pushes 2morow into next week, next week becomes a month from now... C where this is going. Recognize whats going on now. Do something about it now, if you do then yesterday will be just fine and 2morow will take care of itself, when the time comes. If it comes "Time is but an illusion. Death is but

a window, or a door, (depending on how you want/choose to look at it) I'll be back, just as I've been here b4. Not as I am, but exactly as I chose 2 be. K Sun, Son!"

-The God that lives in Me
The God that IS Me
The God that I AM -

* God, as is unde~~r~~rstood by most MEN today, is but an illusion, much the same as "TIME". Past, Present & Future. ALL exist in the never ending moment that is now.

I will live! No longer will
I dwell on or concentrate and spend
large amounts of energy on the
concept and realization of "Death"
For all I, or anyone for that matter,
knows I am dead. This, what
we call world, this life (for
all intents and purposes) may
in fact be the after-life that
so many ponder, have pondered,
& will ponder. The world as we
know it may actually be, and as a
matter of fact is heaven and hell
There is no "streets of gold" or
"fire and brimstone" aside from the
reality that we as human beast
create. I will move on, I will
persevere, I know this b/c I am
as much "God" as is this book, the
paper I write on, or the "pen" in
my left hand. "I" will never die
B/c "I" have always been and "I"
always will be.

I can and will have and become all that there is, was, and will be. I am a spirit experiencing what it is I exist in non-physical form as a "man". My consciousness is seeing itself and actualizing and phatoming itself everywhere, at every moment, through everything" that is at all times and all places. The "me" that is Lamon Dennard Davis, is but a conscious awareness of "me" that I am experiencing at this moment The truth that remains to be hidden is that "I" $ "me" $ "us" and "ALL" are but individual components of a much greater and, since detatched, "machine" that is what it is "Life" "EXISTENCE". "BEING" I am a human "BEING"! That is to say, I am a "BEING" that is being human, a word that describes my conscious awarness of self through the physical body and perspective of a carbon-based life form that exist and is acknowledged by my self as an individual intety. w/ 2 arms, legs, eyes, ears, a heart a mind, a body a soul!

I will say they are the words and voice of "God". For a more complex interpretation I will say these words are "mine" They belong to all and belong to no-one. To know myself I have choosen to be "me", to be all and none, to be everything and nothing, to be everyone and no one. In order to life I have choosen to die. I am 2 halfs of the same coin. I am everywhere and nowhere. To be normal, sane, insane, simple, complex, are all truths to the same fact. that all facts are facts, even to those which are not "facts". We recognize patterns to be consistantly repeating chains of events w/out recognizing the uncontrolled nature of what they are. Simplicity is an tool to use. Chaos is an lack of understanding; yet we do recognize its existance w/out attributing it to all instances.
What am I talking about? What does this all mean? Ameant to? Simply this: Nothing is as it appears. Deeper meaning reside at every facet of all there is. I AM TRUE UNBRIDLED CHAOS. I AM MY OWN MEANS TO AN END.

In Between Dreams Waking moments filled w/ doubt and uncertianty. To what or whom do I owe the pleasure, this so called gift of life. It all comes to a crashing hault anyway right? The value placed on life may be seriously over exadurated or grossly unapreciated. I hope to find the answer to a question that I don't know. So you search? And 4 what is it that I am looking? Collective consciousness, univer-soul, the belief that all life spawns $ is connected to something unseen yet undeniably is felt. Instincts and faith. 1 is a given, the other a choice. Even if I have no faith, by saying so ultimatly means I have faith in my lack of faith. I can nt proclaim something w/out having 1st acknowledging it, analyzing it & thusly coming to a conclusion about it. The wonders of being a child, not knowing what all this is but yerning to know more or as much as possible about it. Somewhere in these words, in my mind and heart lies the answer, but how to recognize it....

Dreams, Reality

Conscious, Subconscious

Electrical symbols interpreted by the brain. What if all my waking moments are actually dreams. What if my dreams are my reality. What if this is hell? What if this is heaven?

March 31, 2006

Ring, Ring goes the phone. Knock, Knock at the door
And for what purpose? To what means? Everywhere
there are questions. In even fewer places there are
answers. I typically am a creature of the night.
Even as a small child my favorite color was black
Is that a good or a bad thing? Keeping in mind that
such concepts are simply a matter of perspective,
I guess the question should be is that good or bad to
or for me. All of existance is 1 half of 1 whole so
why should it matter what half we live on? "with
out evil there would be no good so it must be good
to be evil sometimes" -Satan South Park The Movie
What is the purpose of such a question is the question.
Every man, woman, and child has the option and freedom
of choice to gravitate toward either the positive or negative
which are just terms used to identify & distinguish
2 opposite forces of nature. The problem rather the
issue that presents itself is that of morals and
ethics. Certin activities and walks of live lend
themselves to be scrutinized by these rules and
beliefs of how we as human beings should conduct
ourselves. Others do not. Killing, stealing, abuse,
these can and cannot be catorgorized according to
these "morals" and "ethics". A man should not kill But
at the same time man kills all the time. To kill a spider
or roach in a home is socialy acceptable by the vast
majority. To kill an intruder in your home is too,

depending on the situation. To kill a man who kills other men
has been deemed acceptable by the powers that be.
a spider has the potential to do harm to the inhabities of
a domicile, yet most of the time the spider in all actuality
has yet to do that, but we percieve a threat and act on
the notion of self preservasion and the prevention of the
possibly inevitable actions of a living creature that
technically has done no "wrong". In fact the spider
has, w/out the knowledge of its murderer, done that
individual more "good" in the home than "bad",
killing and eating other "pest". The spider did not moralize
the actions it did, the spider simply fullfilled its
instincual urges to satisfy its own hunger. People
kill the spider out of fear, or b/c it "looks scary". Motives
are logical explinations or justifications for an action. A
criminals' motive to do something that society has
determined a crime are only taken into account to establish
a bases for dealing out the proper punishment for commiting
said "crime". Men have a voice. Men can express their emotion
w/ a complex system of modified sounds produced w/ the
vocal cords that we posses. Yet we still have no true grasp
of what it is we truly feel and do. What we say & what
we do often times differ. "Thou shalt not kill" is what
we say and believe. Yet what we do is vastly to the
contrary. Peace and love are words that we say and
states of being that we claim to wish to achieve, yet
how do we know what peace and love really are?
Individual perception is what makes anything right
or wrong, good or bad, true or false. 2+2=4 is
a true statement, in certin instances and circumstances
2 bullets + 2 people may equal 2 dead people, it may not

*action, rationalization, beliefs, these are the variables that must be taken into account b4 a result can come into existance whats the point? This world, any world is, was, & forever will be full of non-constents. Nothing is set. There is in all actuality no such thing as constant. Life and death are constant only to an extent. we percieve that the end of life is death only b/c No one (except [supposedly] Jesus Christ) has died & come back. Religion

makes an attempt to spell out the after life with its own version of what waits for us once the spirit leaves the body. Yet what mention is there of plants and animals and that which is percieved to never be alive in the 1st place? Some say those things have no spirit, no soul. But what of the rock? A rock is simply tightly compacted condensed forums of matter. Matter is simply that, tightly packed condensed forums of atoms. Atoms are simply what? Tiny bunches of light energy. And energy, as it is believed to be, can not be created or destroyed. So by this rational the term and belief of an "after-life" is false and inacurate. The life one lives while in cased in its biological, organic shell can in fact "end" when the life force vacates the vessel the energy itself does not cease to be. The force that binds the rock, that binds the atoms to form molecules, that binds molecules to cells, the force that binds cells, tissue, organs, systems, and organiziems doesnt simply stop doing what it does when the body ceases to function, yes those coagulation of individual parts does break down & decompose, but there is and always will be something left over. A corpse, ash, fossil fuel, whatever, the shell doesnt simply vanish into thin air. Life and death can not be separated. The distinction btwn the two is superficial at best. All is life and all is death.

Evolution Revolution. I have to take back somethin I previously said. "There is no such thing as constant" The fact that there is no constent is the 1 true constant. At least as far as this world and we as life forms on this plane that we call earth are concerned. We are constantly moving, changing, becoming more then what we were a moment ago. Every day we get a little bit more information, a little bit more evolved. Toward what I'm not sure. Progress does not imply a better state of being, but simply a progression toward something new.

"Loving someonebody dont make them love you"

— Jack Johnson

I can do all that I can to find love, make love a reality in my life, other lives, life in general. But me loving is only a step, alone like an offering, to be accepted. To show love, to give love, to be a loving person is only an invitation for someone or something else to love. Without love we wouldn't know what hate is, and vice versa. Without someone or something else to show us what love is, we can't in turn show or embody that concept. If hate is all we know, how can one show love? If all that we exhibit is the opposite of love, how is it that one can expect to be shown, experience love. Love is an emotion, an invisible entity that can only be described or personified through action.

Gotta go to
work
Love
Mama [illegible]

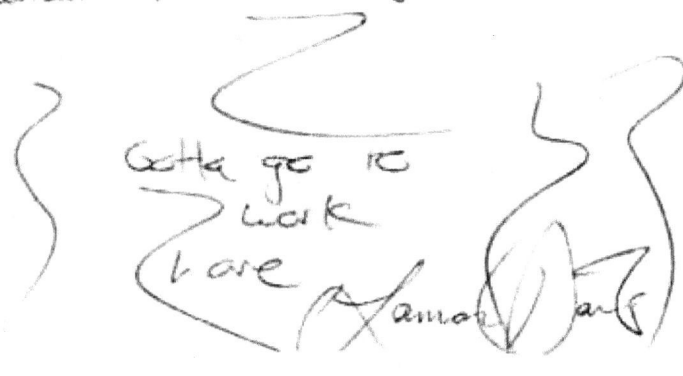

In order to grow, to evolve mentally and spiritualy, one has to come to certain realizations. Certain aspects of life need to be accepted, recognized and delt w/. I can control my own life and no one elses. Things that happen are a result of my actions My emotional state is under my control. I interpreate events, evaluate them and decide (based on past experiences) upon an emotional response. If what I view is negative then w/in me a negative state will be created. Acceptance of the humans free will and a lack of control is one thing. But to be self destructive is my own doing. Giving in to temptation, attempting to aleaviate(SP) my percieved pain my "self medicating" Only hurts me further and creates dependance and addiction In order for me to grow I have to deal w/ life w/ love. Believe in it, embody it. Become it. I can't do that if I am 4ever running from life. Dwelling on my own demise only perpetuates the cyle of negativity. I can not hope to be dead in order to feel good in this life.

I wonder what it is exactly that I am ment to
do. Perhaps nothing. The question is not one of
choice. If there is a task for this life of mine
I whole heartedly accept, which is probably why
Im here in the 1st place. A part of me that existed
b4 birth agreed to be born in order to do something
here on Earth. The problem is my biological
mechinizim lacks the details of said mission. Somewhere
btwn death and life I have 4gotten what Im
suppose to do. My duty now is to merge the body
w/ the mind w/ the soul, which most likely still
retains that knowledge. That fact was also most
likely explained to me b4 arriving. What sort of
thing is so important that I would agree to it, yet
knowing step into this jungle that we call life or being
alive as a man. There are tools here, skills that are
learned, even instincts coded into the DNA. Yet the
thing to do w/ them escapes me. Or perhaps Im
insane. And everything I just said is entirely
fictional. Time will tell. Tick tock

Blank pages lie b4 me beaconing,
yearning to be filled, much like the void of space
But Y ? The purpose of the page is clear, it is
blank so that it may be filled. But what is the
reason 4 the blankness of the mind? Is it not
the same as the page. Now call into question
the content w/ which the mind as well as the
page are filled. A blank mind is filled w/ facts
gatherd on the road of life, then the pages are
filled w/ the facts gatherd from the mind.
Yet the mind uses information gathred from
the environment from which it has been placed,
reassembles, reconfigures, rearranges them and
forms new facts that are placed on the blank
page. The world fills the mind, The mind
fills the page, the page is now used to
fill new minds or even the 1 from which
the words on the page came. The mind moves
faster then both the mouth and the eye. Sometimes
the mind and hand create w/out conscious
awareness of the master. I have written
things, then gone back and read them only
to find myself in aww of what I have
read.

Temporarily insane? Maybe, Perhaps or indiffinatly ingenious? Tell me the diffrence. Show me the world that is or live in the world that isn't. Red or blue pill? Do you enjoy the tumble?

Tumble, tumble, rumble, rumble.

Braind my damage. I think not yet I think, therefor I am but what is a man, a complicated conglomeration of sand. The serpent shall feast on the dust of the land forever & forever until forever meets its end. Thats funny, the end of forever. I bet it'll take forever to get there! Lets race! 1st one to the edge of the universe gets a cookie, maybe even a pat on the back! Sears cheers queers

Millennia is simpley multiple years

walking a trail of tears, its too hot, time to switch gears.

Did you ever imagine what life would be like when life ceases to exist? Existance is futile when the inevidability of death looms overhead like a shadow or scrupulous looking characters that dwell w/in them, call them home, find comfort w/in the abyss that is the absortion of all visible wavelengths of light. Right? or perhaps not, or perhaps true. who r u? what it do! Pimpin! Insanity is lacking the necessary tools & equipment & physical expressions of abstract, intangible & irrationale behavior & thought processes. Yet an answer for all that is it is it as instictualy absent as my have been programed and conditioned to accept as reality. Reality? Reality! Realestate for sale, acution of forecloser.

A broken will to be self drivin. An unyielding
relentless desire to be all that one can be. A
so-called lesser form of life seems to exhibit
peace, bliss & serenity, to such a degree that
one could only dream to achieve. Plants, animals
insects move, live & grow w/out complaint or
defiance to their natural instincts. They just
"exist" and live & don't wonder why. They, some
would say, accept the fact that they are alive,
do what they have to do, and survive b/c thats
why they're here, to survive, to live, flourish,
and multiply. Not having the cognitive ability
and higher

I think, therefore I am? or I Am, therfore I think. Which is true? Can both be true simultanously? Can one be alive yet dead all at the same time, w/in the same moment? Am I living to die, or dying to live? I care but I don't. Trying to live in this world, this life forces one to make determinations about certain facts of life. But ? Self preservation is argreed upon by most as the most important "thing" to do. Ultimatly, all we do is in the name of that concept. But what of entertainment. It is not necessary for survival to be entertained, yet what is life w/out entertainment. The fullfillment of desires is what we live for. Or do we simply desire to be fullfilled? Questions bring about answers, but answers only bring about more questions. The more we learn, the more we realize we don't know. Do we look to the micro, or the macro? Do we search w/in or w/out our own selves. What is w/in is reflected in what is w/out. Looking through a telescope is fundamentally no diffrent then looking through a microscope. Both allow us to see more then what we could see before. Whats out there thats so important? Whats in there thats so relevant? Where does it end? Does it end? Do we want it to end? From the depths of the imagination we manifest into existence innumberable supposed original thoughts, ideas, creations, inventions. Yet if we all imagine, if we all dream, what then can we claim to be original? If I put to lines together and form a "+" & you do the same but form an "X", how can either of us claim to be original when we all have the same material to work with? How can anyone be more or less right or wrong then the next person when everything exist and is accessable to everyone else. Things exist b/c we say they do, or do they? None of us was here when it all began, or where we? If God is within us, & throughout us, how can we say that we are not God? Our, rather most concepts of God puts between us some sort of separation. When we do good its of God, when we do bad, its not? How can God be all & everything if we distinguish & label things "of God" & "not of God" That in itself negates the omnipresent, all encompasing Christian, western philosophy concept of God.

I think it is time for a drastic re-apraisal of the situation. Perhaps peace is so difficult to obtain b/c we divide everything into pieces, losing site of the whole. Often we forget. Often we neglect, more often then not we decieve our selves. "Everything" is broad & untangible to conceive, yet we know of, have conceptualized, and recognized the there is an "everything."

I had to sit for a moment and clarify the rantings of my own psyche. I'm not sure if what goes on in my mind is the typical happings of the species. I'm not so abnormal to be comitted, for all intents & purposes. I'm above average intellegent and fully functional. But thats b/c I know how to answer questions. What am I?, who am I, and when will it all make sense?

Its funny, b/c nobody will ever laugh in the way that I laughed, b/c of the same reason, or under the same siccumstances, or for the same reason that I laughed.

one might see the same wave but from a different angle, and claim the same perspectivo, but that just aint the truth now is it?

call
tonight
right

I know I wrote it, I was there, but not all there. & go back and see truths that I have written but have yet to know is amazing!

"There's a difference btwn knowing the path and walking the path"

"From the mouths of babes"

Life is so simple as a child, the world is filled w/ endless possibility and wonder. The process of growing old constricts the mind and spirit. This is how I know I am not a child. Life is no longer simple. Possibility now has its limitations. I can no longer make everything anything b/c I have programed to think & "know" that things are "things". But all is not lost there exist the potential to move back to that mind set that I can do anything, be anything. It takes more work, but it is possible. Stoping change is the only impossibility. Evolution is a never ending process. People are creatures of habit and like to be in familiar patterns and ways of being.

"Which is the most universal concept: fear or lazyness?"

www.ingramcontent.com/pod-product-compliance
Lightning Source LLC
Chambersburg PA
CBHW051319120626
46547CB00015B/2309
*9781963250350*